TAKE-OFF!

Materials

Wood

Chris Oxlade

Heinemann
LIBRARY

www.heinemann.co.uk/library
Visit our website to find out more information about Heinemann Library books.

To Order:
☎ Phone 44 (0) 1865 888066
▤ Send a fax to 44 (0) 1865 314091
▭ Visit the Heinemann Library Bookshop at www.heinemann.co.uk/library to browse our catalogue and order online.

First published in Great Britain by Heinemann Library, Halley Court, Jordan Hill, Oxford OX2 8EJ,
a division of Reed Educational and Professional Publishing Ltd.
Heinemann is a registered trademark of Reed Educational and Professional Publishing Ltd.

OXFORD MELBOURNE AUCKLAND JOHANNESBURG BLANTYRE
GABORONE IBADAN PORTSMOUTH (NH) USA CHICAGO

Designed by Storeybooks
Originated by Dot Gradations Ltd
Printed by South China Printing in Hong Kong/China

ISBN 0 431 03740 X (hardback)   ISBN 0 431 03745 0 (paperback)
06 05 04 03 02   06 05 04 03 02
10 9 8 7 6 5 4 3 2 1   10 9 8 7 6 5 4 3 2 1

British Library Cataloguing in Publication Data
    Oxlade, Chris
    Wood. – (Materials)
    1. Wood
    I. Title
    620.1'2

Acknowledgements
Corbis pp.19, /Jack Fields p.29, /Darrell Gulin p.24, /Barry Lewis p.13, /Richard T. Nowitz p.22; Holt p.6; Hutchison p.23; Oxford Scientific Films pp.4, 9, 10, /Michael Fogden p.25; Photodisc pp.15, 26, 27; Still Pictures /Mark Edwards p.11, /Hartmut Schwarzbach p.12; The Builder Group p.8; Trip/Viesti Collection p.18; Tudor Photography pp.5, 7, 14, 17, 20, 21.

Cover photograph reproduced with permission of Robert Harding Picture Library.

Every effort has been made to contact copyright holders of any material reproduced in this book. Any omissions will be rectified in subsequent printings if notice is given to the publishers.

Contents

You can find words shown in bold, **like this**, in the glossary.

What is wood?

branch

trunk

Wood comes from trees.

Wood is renewable. We need never run out of wood if we always plant new trees for the future.

Wood is a **natural** material. It comes from the trunks and branches of trees. People cut trees down and chop them into pieces so that they can use the wood.

Wood is an important material. People make many different things from wood. Toys, ornaments, furniture and houses can all be made from wood.

All these things are made from wood.

vase   bowl   pepper grinder   metronome

lidded box   animals   figure

Different woods

rings   bark

The trunk of a tree has lines or rings in it.

The trunks and branches of a tree are covered in **bark**. Underneath the bark the wood is **grainy**. Different woods are different colours.

Do you know that you can tell the age of a tree by counting the rings in its trunk? Work out how old the tree in the photo is.

Beech trees have wood which is very hard
and heavy. Balsa trees have soft, light wood.

Timber trees are either soft wood or hard wood.

beech

balsa

Strong and bendy

The inside of this building is made with thick pieces of wood.

wood

Most kinds of wood are strong when you try to squash or bend them. Hard wood is stronger than soft wood.

Hard wood trees are mainly deciduous. This means they lose their leaves in the winter.

The young, thin branches of some trees are very bendy. They can bend almost in half without snapping. This can be very useful for making things such as baskets and fences.

The branches of young trees bend in the wind.

Rotting and burning

floorboards

These wooden floorboards are rotting away because they are damp.

When branches break off a tree and fall to the ground, the wood begins to rot away. Any wood that gets wet for a time will soon start to rot.

Wood does not **melt** when it is heated. But when it gets very hot, it burns. In many parts of the world, people collect wood to use as a **fuel** for cooking or for keeping warm.

Wood is a useful fuel for cooking.

wood fire   cooking pot

11

Growing wood

felled tree

The trees are felled, or cut down, when they are big enough.

Most wood for building and making furniture comes from fir trees. The trees are grown for their wood.

In North America, people who **fell** trees are called lumberjacks.

After the trees are cut down, the branches are chopped off to leave a trunk. The trunks are carried to a **sawmill** where they are cut into large planks.

The trunks are cut into planks of wood.

sawmill

planks

tree trunks

Working with wood

saw   drill

wood shavings

Carpenters use tools such as saws and drills.

Wood is a useful material because it is easy to cut
into shapes and make into things. A **carpenter**
is a person who makes useful things around the
house, such as doors, from wood.

This building is made of wood. First the carpenter cuts the wood into different lengths and shapes with an electric saw. Then he joins the pieces together with bolts and screws.

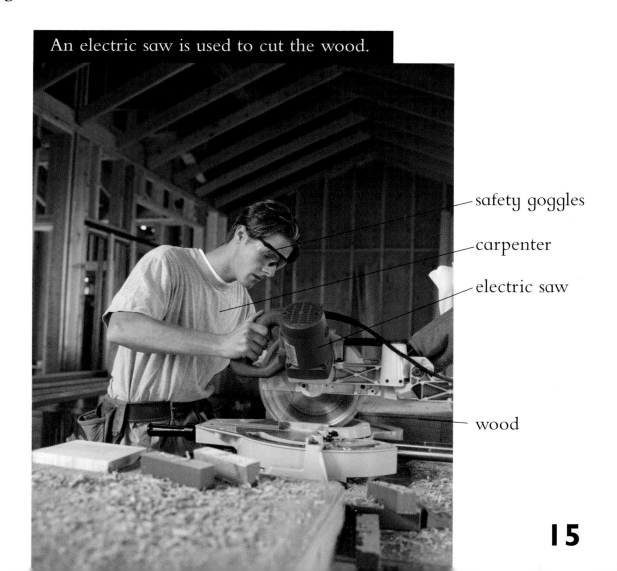

An electric saw is used to cut the wood.

safety goggles

carpenter

electric saw

wood

Sheets of wood

Sheets of wood are called boards.
Chipboard is made of small chunks of
wood. The chunks are mixed with glue
and squeezed together until the glue
sets hard.

wood chips

Chipboard is
made from
wood chips.

Plywood is another kind of board. It is made by gluing thin sheets of hard wood on top of each other.

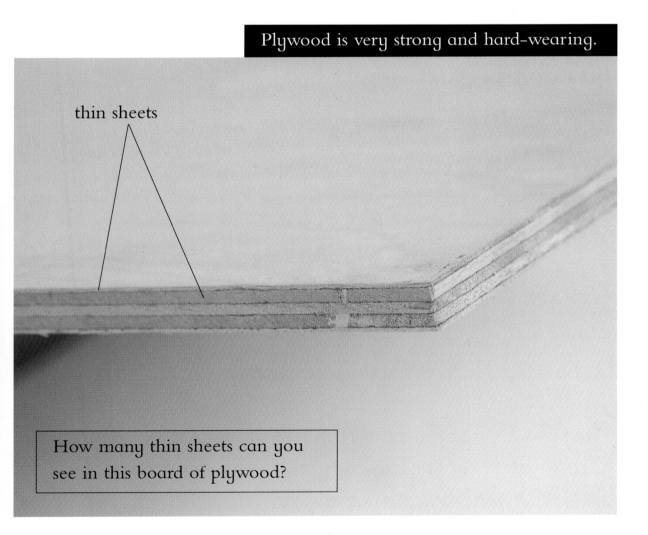

Plywood is very strong and hard-wearing.

thin sheets

How many thin sheets can you see in this board of plywood?

Caring for wood

Wood must be painted to protect it from rotting.

painted wood

painter

Wood that is used outdoors must be protected from rotting. Two or three layers of oily paint stop water reaching the wood's surface.

Fence posts are dipped in special **chemicals** before they are put in the ground. These chemicals are called preservatives.

Preservatives prevent the posts from rotting.

fence posts

Creosote is a popular preservative for using on fence posts. Creosote is a black, oily liquid made from coal tar.

Looking good

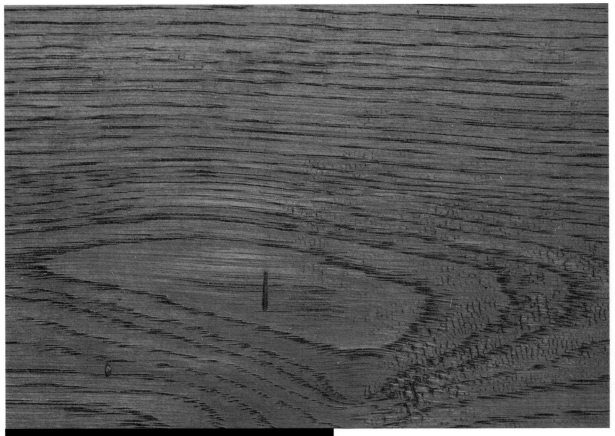

Polishing wood brings out its grain.

The grainy patterns in wood are often beautiful. They are used for decoration. The wood is made smooth with **sandpaper** and then polished to make the **grain** show up.

Pieces of wood with different colours can be put next to each other to make patterns.

A veneer is a thin piece of fine wood glued on to a less expensive piece. Some furniture is made with veneers. The furniture will look good but will be cheaper to make!

wood pieces

This pattern has been made from small pieces of wood.

Local wood

tree trunks

log cabin

This log cabin was built from whole tree trunks.

People who live in places where there are large forests use wood for almost everything they make.

People who live by rivers in the world's **rainforests** make boats from tree trunks. They dig out the centre of the trunk with axes.

These boats are called dug-out canoes.

paddle

dug-out canoe

23

Animal wood users

Beavers have sharp teeth to gnaw through tree trunks.

Like humans, many animals use wood as a building material. Beavers cut down trees with their sharp front teeth and use them to build **dams** and homes called lodges.

24

Many birds make nests from dead branches and twigs they collect from the ground. Bowerbirds are expert builders. The male bird builds something called a bower to attract a **mate**.

This bower has been made from twigs and grasses.

twigs

bowerbird

grasses

Saving the rainforests

About 40 per cent of the world's plants and animals live in rainforests!

Every day thousands of rainforest trees are destroyed for their wood.

Thousands of different plants grow in a **rainforest**. The trees are some of the tallest and oldest in the world. Many birds and animals live in them.

One way to help save the rainforests from being cut down is to plant more trees. If we get our wood from these planted trees, we do not need to cut down the rainforests.

Planting more trees could help save the rainforests.

forester

sapling

27

Fact file

- Wood is a **natural** material. It comes from trees.

- Wood from a tree feels rough. It has lines in it called the **grain**.

- Woods from different kinds of trees are different colours.

- Some kinds of wood are heavy and hard. Some are light and soft.

- Old, thick pieces of wood are stiff. Young, thin pieces of wood are bendy.

- Wood burns when it is heated up.

- Wood floats in water.

- Wood is not attracted by **magnets**.

- **Electricity** and heat do not flow through wood.

Would you believe it?

There is an aircraft built in 1947 called the *Spruce Goose*. It is the biggest aircraft in the world, even bigger than a modern jumbo jet. It is made completely from wood!

The wooden *Spruce Goose*.

Glossary

a
b
c
d
e
f
g
h
i
j
k
l
m
n
o
p
q
r
s
t
u
v
w
x
y
z

bark   outer layer of wood on a tree trunk or a branch

carpenter   person who works with wood to make things

chemicals   special materials that are used in factories and homes to do many jobs, including cleaning and protecting

dam   structure that holds back water to make a lake

electricity   form of energy. We use electricity to make electric machines work.

felled   cut or knocked down

fuel   substance that people burn to make heat or light, or to make engines work. Wood is a fuel. So are gas and petrol.

grain   pattern of rings and lines inside wood

magnet   object that pulls steel and iron objects towards it

mate   male or female animal in a pair of animals that have babies together

melt   turn from solid to liquid

natural   comes from plants, animals or the rocks in the earth

rainforest   thick, jungly forest where lots of rain falls

sandpaper   tough paper with grains of sand glued to it. Rubbing wood with sandpaper makes the wood smooth.

sawmill   factory where trees are cut into planks with powerful saws

More books to read

Plants: British Trees by Angela Royston, Heinemann Library, 2000

Science Explorers: Wood A & C Black, 1999

Science Files: Wood by Steve Parker, Heinemann Library, 2001

Shooting Stars: Material Matters by Robert Roland, Belitha Press, 2002

Index